STUDY GUIDE

Defending Your Faith

An Overview of Classical Apologetics

R.C. Sproul

LIGONIER MINISTRIES
Renew your Mind.

LIGONIER.ORG | 800-435-4343

Copyright © 2001, 2010 Ligonier Ministries
421 Ligonier Court, Sanford, FL 32771
E-mail: info@ligonier.org
All rights reserved.
No reproduction of this work without permission.
Printed in the United States of America.

1

Introduction to Apologetics

MESSAGE INTRODUCTION

Do you know what you believe and why you believe it? If you are like most Christians, you are not as certain of the answer as you would like to be. In this lecture, R.C. explains that the science of apologetics is designed to aid Christians in the joyful task and responsibility of defending their faith.

LEARNING OBJECTIVES

1. To understand the history and definition of apologetics.
2. To be encouraged to observe and imitate the Bible's apologetical methods.

QUOTATIONS AND THOUGHTS

Logos: Greek, meaning "word" or "reason". In biblical Greek, especially in the book of John, it often refers to the Second Person of the Trinity. In early Greek philosophy, it was used to denote the supreme ordering force of the universe.

LECTURE OUTLINE

I. What is apologetics?
    a. Apologetics is devoted to promoting an intellectual defense for truth claims, in this case the truth claims of the Christian faith.
    b. It has no reference to apologizing for something you did wrong, though it comes from the same Greek root.

II. The Bible and Apologetics
   a. First Peter 3:15 says, "But sanctify the Lord God in your hearts, and always be ready to give a defense to everyone who asks you a reason for the hope that is in you, with meekness and fear; having a good conscience, that when they defame you as evildoes, those who revile your good conduct in Christ may be ashamed."
   b. The positive reason for apologetics is the sanctification of the Christian, but the negative one is to make non-Christians ashamed of attacking the Christian faith.
   c. Justin Martyr wrote "The Apology."
      i. It was a response to the charges of sedition, cannibalism, and atheism by the Roman authorities.
      ii. In 2001 John Ashcroft was forced to make a similar "apology" when he remarked, "We in America have no King but Jesus."
      iii. Christians have always responded intellectually and Biblically to the various cultural and political movements that questioned the reality of the Christian faith.
   d. The *Logos* and Apologetics
      i. Early apologists appealed to the *logos* concept to explain the nature of Jesus to the Greek culture.
      ii. *Logos* was used in philosophical discussions among the Stoics and Heraclitians to denote the primary organizing force of the universe.
      iii. The Apostle John picks up on this and uses this word to explain the nature of Christ to a primarily Greek-thinking culture. But he fills it with Hebrew content and theology.
      iv. There are significant points of contact between the Christian and non-Christian world, in this case, a semantic one
      v. Sensing this connection, Gordon Clark translates the first verse of John's Gospel as, "In the beginning was logic, and logic was with God, and logic was God. And the logic became flesh and dwelt among us."

III. It is the contributions of the early apologists in interacting with surrounding cultural ideas that provide the first clues for the content of apologetics. The rest of this course will explore the implications and applications of this example.

STUDY QUESTIONS

1. What is the definition of the word "apologetics"?

2. What two Biblical passages have impacted the study of apologetics? Why?

3. What was the use of the word *logos* in

a. Normal Greek?

b. Greek philosophy?

c. John's Gospel?

DISCUSSION QUESTIONS

1. Read 1 Peter 3:15. What can we learn about the purpose of apologetics from this passage?

2. Looking at Acts 17, is there a clear distinction between doing apologetics and evangelism in Paul's preaching? What are the differences and similarities?

3. What are three points of contact with Christianity in your culture? Think of art, politics, vocational issues, etc.

4. Make at least three goals—one intellectual, one emotional, and one kinetic or "doing" to give you direction as you prepare to take this course.

    a. I want to learn. . . .

    b. I want to feel. . . .

    c. I want to do. . . .

2

Why Apologetics?

MESSAGE INTRODUCTION

Apologetics is positive and negative. It sets forth the reasons for belief, and it tears down the opposing arguments. But if you can't argue anyone into the kingdom, why do it in the first place? Let's find out from Dr. Sproul.

LEARNING OBJECTIVES

1. To understand the offensive and defensive sides of apologetics.
2. To understand the difference between proof and persuasion.
3. To learn to appreciate and rely on the Scriptures and the rich tradition of apologetics as we confront the challenges of today.

QUOTATIONS AND THOUGHTS

credulous

Obstreperous (adj.): noisily resisting control or defying commands [from Latin, *obstreperous*, noisy]

St. Thomas Aquinas (1225–1274): Scholastic philosopher and theologian, born in Roccasecca, Italy. Most significant pre-Trent Catholic scholar other than Augustine. Three years after his death, a number of his views were condemned by Catholic authorities in Paris and Oxford, but in 1323, he was canonized by Pope John XXII, and in 1879, Pope Leo XIII issued an encyclical commending all his works to Catholic scholars.

LECTURE OUTLINE

I. Apologetics: Positive and Negative
   a. We must state our position, positively affirming what the Christian church believes, if we are challenged. This can require much patience.

Why Apologetics?

obstreperous

    b. We should also correct or tear down the false assumptions and irrationality present in other systems.

II. Where does apologetics start?
    a. Some, like R.C., argue that apologetics starts with the <u>existence of God.</u> Others say that you start with Scripture, or with history.
    b. All apologetics systems that have any merit must affirm the depravity of man and the necessity of the <u>Holy Spirit's work</u> in conversion.

III. Why do apologetics?
    a. To obey the Scriptures—see 1 Peter 3:15. *Always be prepared to make a defense to anyone who asks you for a reason for the hope that is in you.*
    b. To shame obstreperous non-Christians, as John Calvin stated. *(noisy)*
    c. "The fool has said in his heart, 'There is no God.'"
    d. Christians should not surrender rationality and scientific inquiry to the secular world. The commonsense tools of learning can be used to corroborate the truth claims of Christianity.

IV. Proof and Persuasion
    a. Proof can be offered, even <u>irrefutable proof,</u> but it does not necessarily lead <u>to a change in belief.</u>
    b. The Holy Spirit causes the acquiescence into the soundness of the argument for the truth claims of the Christian faith. <u>The role of the apologist is not persuasion, but proof.</u>
    c. Illustration: Charlie the Skeptic
    d. "Those convinced against their will hold their first opinion still."
    e. While we are not able to change minds, <u>we are able to give a faithful defense and thus add credibility to the Christian faith.</u>

STUDY QUESTIONS

- Do we consider ourselves to be reformed.

1. What are the positive and negative sides of apologetics?
Positive – affirm Christian religion. Negative – tear down false assumptions, protecting against ridicule. It is God's command.
2. Why do apologetics if people's minds are changed only by God?
3. What is the difference between proof and persuasion?
Proof – providing facts
Persuasion – changed mind

DISCUSSION QUESTIONS

1. In the context of arguing for the Christian faith, why does it take a miracle to persuade someone of his error? See Ephesians 1-2 for some hints. *Need the Holy Spirit.*
2. *Credulous.* Were you easily convinced of the rationality of the Christian faith, or were you more like "Charlie the Skeptic"? What do you do when someone is seemingly invincible to your arguments, no matter how good they are?

Letters from a Skeptic   C.S. Lewis, Mere Christianity

3. Do you know someone personally who excels at apologetics? What is it that makes him or her so good?

4. Are there people you know who are asking many questions about your faith? Pray for them and yourself as you end this session.

Andrew Langseth
Josh Kruger —
    explains —
        + no condescension
        + real life examples
        + knows exactly where to find it.

Nate

3

Pre-Evangelism

MESSAGE INTRODUCTION

God uses many means to draw people unto Himself. Not just a preaching of the Gospel, or Bible study, or prayer, or baptism, though those are the ordinary means He uses. He also used the godly disputation of apologetics as a way of extending an outer call to rebellious mankind. How can you participate in God's work in this area? Dr. Sproul explains how.

LEARNING OBJECTIVES

1. To understand the need to study philosophy.
2. To understand the presuppositions of Reformed theology concerning conversion.
3. To understand the importance of the public nature of the foundational events of the New Testament (Christ's life, death and resurrection).

QUOTATIONS AND THOUGHTS

When a Christian presents the good news of Jesus Christ, he is preaching treason in the Devil's kingdom (Doug Barnett).

Assensus: Latin, "assent" or "agreement." Scholars distinguish three degrees of assent: *firmitas, certitude,* and *evidential*. The first is assent based on the authority of the person who tells you. The second is agreement based on accepted testimony. The third is assent based on evidence, from either personal sense-experience or reason. Apologetics seeks the third type of assent.

LECTURE OUTLINE

I. Beware vs. Aware
   a. Many refuse to study classical theology or philosophy because they are afraid of being influenced.

b. But how can you beware of something you are not aware of in the first place? Thus, some level of familiarity is necessary when avoiding sin or the influence of sinful ideologies.
c. We cooperate with the Holy Spirit in the proclamation and defense of Christianity.

II. Pre-Evangelism and Apologetics
   a. The role of apologetics in pre-evangelism is to promote knowledge of God, but is not contrary to the doctrine of justification by faith alone.
   b. Fides Viva means "a living faith." It is used in context of the discussion of the nature of saving faith. In this case:
      i. *Noticia*: Know what data?
      ii. *Assensus*: Affirm what propositions?
      iii. *Fiducia*: Trust or love whom?
      iv. The first two can be accomplished by demons. The latter is done only by the regenerate, through the Holy Spirit alone. The first two are the role of apologetics.
   c. Fideism, or the belief that someone should take a blind leap of faith into Christianity, is dangerous. We are called to leap from darkness to light, not from darkness to darkness.
   d. The greatest mysteries of the Christian faith were done in the open. This is why we can do apologetics—we can announce clear, public evidence to the world.

III. Conclusion: God commands us to do our homework, that He may use those means to draw people unto Himself. Part of the way in which we give people more certitude about the Christian claims is to point out the public nature of Christianity.

STUDY QUESTIONS

1. Does giving reasons for the Christian faith counter the work of the Holy Spirit? Why?

2. How does apologetics aid pre-evangelism?

3. What are the three components of Biblical faith?

DISCUSSION QUESTIONS

1. Do you know someone who has *noticia* and/or *assensus* but no *fiducia*? What is his or her greatest need? What can you do to help?

2. In a postmodern culture, in which certitude about God is downplayed, how do we defend against fideism?

3. What philosophers have you read? Make it your goal to become familiar with the works of a major philosopher, like Plato, Kant, the pre-Socratic philosophers, Nietzche, or G.W.F. Hegel. Also study one influential philosopher with Christian presuppositions, such as Augustine, Aquinas, Kierkegaard, George Berkeley, or Gordon Clark.

4

Four Steps Backward

MESSAGE INTRODUCTION

Epistemology is the study of how people know what they know. There have been many approaches to this, and some utterly fail to give any certitude to us in the areas of faith. Why do some theories of knowledge fail and others succeed? And why is this important to Christianity? This study begins to answer that question by establishing four nonnegotiable presuppositions about knowledge.

LEARNING OBJECTIVES

1. To value the science of epistemology.
2. To become familiar with the terms surrounding elementary epistemology.
3. To apply the four basic principles of knowledge to our own ideas and the ideas presented to us by the world.

QUOTATIONS AND THOUGHTS

Argument: An argument consists of one or more premises and one conclusion. A premise is a statement (a sentence that is either true or false) that is offered in support of the claim being made, which is the conclusion. The latter is also an idea that is either true or false.

I'm from Missouri, and we don't believe it unless we see it! (Anonymous Missourian)

LECTURE OUTLINE

I. What is epistemology?
    a. How do we know what we know? How can we verify or falsify claims of truth?

b. Do we know only through senses or mind? Or formal proofs, such as mathematics?
c. As this relates to apologetics, it raises the question of what the "real" way is to prove the existence of God, the way that carries the most certitude.

II. Epistemology and Apologetics
   a. How do the opponents of theism establish their negative case against the Christian faith? Almost all attack four foundational principles of knowing.
      i. Law of Non-Contradiction
      ii. Law of Causality
      iii. Basic Reliability of Sense Perception
      iv. Analogical Use of Language
   b. Certain presuppositions or assumptions must be analyzed concerning these four ideas. We do this by asking:
      i. What premises are asserted by opponents?
      ii. What premises are assumed by Scripture?
      iii. If these four concepts are negotiable, then not only theology but all sciences are rendered moot, or, at best, unreliable.

III. Conclusion: There is an analogy between Creator and creature that makes the epistemological assumptions of God our own.

STUDY QUESTIONS

1. What is epistemology? Why is it important to apologetics? *[handwritten: Subdivision of philosophy / the study of how people know what they know. / must manifest]*
2. Name three famous atheists. *[handwritten: John Stuart Mill, Karl Marx, Jean-Paul Sartre, Albert Camus, Walter Kaufman]*
3. Name the four assumptions necessary for rational communication. *[handwritten: 1) The Law of Non Contradiction 2) The Law of Causality "cause + effect" 3) the basic reliability of sense perception 4) The analogical use of language.]*

DISCUSSION QUESTIONS

1. Since these four epistemological assumptions are foundational, there are no precise supporting Scriptures for them—foundations rest upon themselves, not other structures. Which one of these assumptions is most doubted by you and your culture?

2. What are some ways to proceed in an evangelistic situation if someone denies one of these points? *[handwritten: What point are they denying? Connect them with an expert. Dig into the Scripture to find truth.]*

3. Look at Romans 11:33, Isaiah 40:13, and Jeremiah 23:18. Do these passages contradict any of these assumptions? What do they indicate?

[Editor's Note: The Law of Contradiction and the Law of Non-Contradiction are the same idea. The terms are interchangeable.]

5

Law of Contradiction

MESSAGE INTRODUCTION

True relativists are a dying breed—literally. You cannot live very long thinking that red lights can mean either stop or go, or that rat poison tastes like chocolate. There are grave natural consequences for embracing relativism on any level, and there are spiritual consequences for being a spiritual relativist as well. The law of contradiction, if true, challenges all types of dangerous relativism.

LEARNING OBJECTIVES

1. To sense the dangers of relativism.
2. To understand the existence of certain self-evident properties or assumptions about logic.
3. To understand that natural relativism and supernatural relativism are equally invalidated by the law of contradiction.

QUOTATIONS AND THOUGHTS

What are the two types of arguments? The two types of arguments are *deductive* and *inductive*. A deductive argument is an argument such that the premises provide complete support for the conclusion. An inductive argument is an argument such that the premises provide (or appear to provide) some degree of support for the conclusion. Deductive arguments prove validity; inductive arguments establish likelihood.

LECTURE OUTLINE

I. What changes have occurred in our society since the mid-sixties?
    a. Assumptions about truth have changed. This led to the book *The Closing of the American Mind* by Alan Bloom. He showed that 95% of high school graduates enter college with a relativistic mind-set.

Closed to objective truth

Law of Contradiction

   b. Bloom said: "Then what happens in the following four years is that those assumptions that they come to college with out of high school are now set in concrete because the academic community in modern America has a mind that is closed to objective truth. Truth is now perceived as being subjective, as a matter of preference."
   c. This is bad news and good news.

II. Aristotle and Logic
   a. Aristotle (384-322 B.C.) developed theories of physics, chemistry, drama, ethics and biology. As he proceeded, he developed theories of logic that we now call Aristotelian logic.
   b. Logic was not a science, but the necessary tool for all scientific inquiry. — *Aristotle*
   c. Illustration: Chalk is NOT chalk — *Violated the law of contradiction*
   d. Illustration: Salt shaker and non-salt shaker
   e. Denials of ideas like the law of contradiction are forced and temporary.

III. Christian Relativism
   a. Karl Barth and Emil Brunner were influenced by the philosophical speculation of Soren Kierkegaard. These men have had a profound impact, bringing relativistic, contradiction-embracing thought into theology.
   b. The Scriptures teach as early as Genesis 3 that God assumed that mankind understood the law of contradiction.
   c. Illustration: Adam as a student of Aristotle and Barth
   d. Christians must embrace logic, ~~the means~~ to measure the relationship between premises and conclusions. — *Jerusalem → Athens*

IV. Conclusion: God has built the human mind to be rational. The word of God is not irrational. It is addressed to creatures who have been given minds that operate from certain principles, the law of contradiction being one of them.

STUDY QUESTIONS

1. What is relativism? — *theory that all people hold their own truth; Truth - black/white thinking*
2. Did Aristotle discover logic? Define "logic." — *defined; NO, discovered rules that were already there - placed by our creator. Measure relationship between premises.*
3. Historically speaking, how did relativism creep into Christian thought?

DISCUSSION QUESTIONS

1. Is relativism as big a problem as R.C. suggests? Do you see ethical, sociological, or educational problems because of relativism?
   — *(Man vs woman)   life vs death*

2. How does an attack on the law of contradiction do damage to Christianity?

3. Morality has a situational component to it: Normally, it is wrong to kill people, but there are some situations in which killing is allowed. Why is this not relativism?

4. Does the existence of mystery and lack of clarity found in the Bible demonstrate limits to logic? Or limits to God's Word? Why or why not?

6

Law of Causality

MESSAGE INTRODUCTION

The second of the four principles of knowledge is the law of causality. This law is defined as "Every effect must have a cause." A right understanding of this law can lead one to the answer to one of the greatest theological questions the seven year old can muster: "Who made God?" A wrong understanding can lead to denying the existence of God. Thus, the importance of this law should not be minimized.

LEARNING OBJECTIVES

1. To see the seriousness of misunderstanding or ignoring this law.
2. To understand the nuances of the word "effect."
3. To understand David Hume's objections to causality.

QUOTATIONS AND THOUGHTS

The mind is good—God put it there. He gave us our heads and it was not his intention that our heads would function just as a place to hang a hat. (A.W. Tozer)

It doesn't take a great mind to be a Christian, but it does take all the mind a man has. (R.C. Raines)

Nothing but faith will ever rectify the mistakes of reason on divine things. (William S. Plumer)

LECTURE OUTLINE

I. Four principles of knowledge are crucial for dialog about God.
   a. Law of non-contradiction
   b. Law of causality

      c. Basic reliability of sense perception
      d. Analogical use of language

II. The Law of Causality
      a. Prior to the Enlightenment (which emerged in 18th-century France), the principle of causality was the foundational and unchallenged argument for the existence of God. Aristotle began this tradition by arguing that God was the "First Cause" or "Unmoved Mover."
      b. Bertrand Russell believed in God as a young man, but after reading John Stuart Mill, who objected to the causal argument for the existence of God, he was convinced otherwise.
      c. But Mill and Russell, great philosophers though they may be, made an error of definition. They believed that using causality as an argument for the existence of God only led to a series of infinite regressions.
      d. They defined the law of causation as, "Everything must have a cause." But the true definition of the law is, "Every effect must have an antecedent cause." The God we claim exists is not an effect; He is uncaused. Thus, He does not require a cause. Therefore, infinite regress does not occur.

III. Understanding Causality
      a. Formal truth and analytical truth
      b. Illustration: A bachelor is an unmarried man.
      c. Formal principles do not directly teach us anything about the real world.
      d. Illustration: Dr. Sproul will not allow for uncaused effects.

IV. Conclusion: Did David Hume destroy causality and therefore causal arguments for the existence of God?

STUDY QUESTIONS

1. What are the four principles of knowledge necessary for dialogue about God (or anything else, for that matter?)

2. Who was one of the first philosophers to argue that the cause of the creation of the world must be explained by the existence of God?

3. What is the "bad" definition of "causality" that confused Mills and Russell, and what is the "good" one? What is the difference?

DISCUSSION QUESTIONS

1. Causality is not just a law—it's a description of how things act. How does the system of morality, and the accompanying rewards and punishments related to good and bad deeds, affirm the law of causality?

2. Causality is a principle that cannot be proved to be true, nor can causality sometimes be determined in certain events. Even after careful study, it is difficult to know why certain things happen. Why believe in a principle like causality when it is so difficult to prove or observe?

3. Christians do not believe in the "Unmoved Mover" of Aristotle. God is alive and active in the universe. But in what way is God unchanging and unmoved?

7
Reliability of Sense Perception

MESSAGE INTRODUCTION

The third of the four principles of knowledge is the reliability of sense perception. The formal questions about the reliability of our senses arise because of Humes's pointing out the limitations of what our senses can know about causality. Practically speaking, those who attempt to deny the basic trustworthiness of our perceptions end up being certified as insane. While our senses are not perfect, they provide true (though limited) information about the universe, or else God would not have the right to judge those who sin against Him. They could simply protest, "How could I have known?"

LEARNING OBJECTIVES

1. To see the seriousness of misunderstanding or ignoring this law.
2. To understand the limits of Hume's objections to common assumptions about causality.
3. To trust that God has not left us without a way to rightly know Him.

QUOTATIONS AND THOUGHTS

What is a fallacy? It is an error in reasoning. This differs from a factual error, which is simply being wrong about the facts. The various descriptions of fallacies are simply different ways in which the premises, true as they may be, do not lead to the conclusion. A conclusion may be true and the premises be true, but the argument may still be bad because it is based on fallacious reasoning.

LECTURE OUTLINE

I. The laws of non-contradiction and causality are two of the four ideas attacked by non-theists.

a. The law of Non-Contradiction is necessary to survive.
b. Causality was most critically attacked by David Hume (1711-1776).

II. David Hume and His "Inquiry"
   a. What we observe when we see things happen are "customary relationships" or "relationships of contiguity."
   b. When one thing follows another, we begin to assume that that which follows is caused by that which preceded. This observation is the kernel of Hume's concerns.
   c. How do we know that some other factor is interceding to create the illusion of a certain cause relating to a certain effect?
   d. Descartes and Spinoza postulated invisible causes to that which could not be empirically observed. Hume's observations were critical to affirming or denying these kinds of speculations.
   e. Illustration: Germs and Spirits

III. Hume and Pool Tables
   a. Hume's most famous illustration of his concerns was from the game of pool.
   b. Does anyone actually see the transfer of force from the cue to the ball? No. We do not truly see causality, but we assume a causal nexus.
   c. Illustration: Roosters and Sunshine
   d. *Post hoc ergo propter hoc*: "After this, therefore because of this."

IV. Did Hume disprove causality?
   a. No. He proved that we cannot know cause and effect with ultimate certitude. But the principle stays intact.
   b. This leads to the third principle that is attacked by non-theists, that of sense perception. Hume reveals that sense perception has limits, but does not destroy the principle.
   c. At best, we are all secondary causes. The power of God is, as Hume speculates, invisible and unseen. The primary cause of all effects is God, and thus His work actually complements Biblical theism rather than destroys it.
   d. Kant affirmed that Hume's findings drove him to attempt to rescue science from skepticism. Kant understood that if Hume had destroyed causality, then not only theism, but all scientific inquiry, was in danger.

V. What is mind?
   a. My senses cannot adequately determine causality (either prove it or see it consistently). But they are the only links I have between the world and the mind. And they are sufficiently powerful enough to assume that they are giving us a true (yet partial) view of reality.
   b. "What is mind? No matter. What is matter? Never mind."

c. The brain gives rise to thinking, but thinking or consciousness itself is not physical.
d. Basic reliability of sense perception must be assumed because those senses are the only way in which the mind can gather data. Peter affirmed this as he reported that early believers were not clinging to clever myths or fables, but to things they had seen with their eyes and heard with their ears.

STUDY QUESTIONS

1. David Hume said that when we see one thing follow another, this is called a _____ relationship.

2. What is the *post hoc, ergo proptor hoc* fallacy? Give one example.

3. What is the connection between the mind and the world?

DISCUSSION QUESTIONS

1. Our senses are limited in many ways. Name three forces or effects that we cannot sense (touch, taste, smell), but that we know exist.

2. The "God of the Gap" theory was frequently used in ancient science. When something was observed for which no cause could be found, it was assumed that God had done it. The person of God filled the gap between facts and the human mind. How is this theory right? How is it wrong?

3. How is R.C.'s explanation of Hume's critique of causality consistent with Christianity?

8

Analogical Language (Part 1)

MESSAGE INTRODUCTION

G.K. Chesterton said, "Christianity has not been tried and found wanting; it has been tried and found difficult." Philosophy has definitely been tried and found wanting, but some of its richest treasures are not lying on the surface. Our study of analogical language is a good opportunity to break a mental sweat for God's glory and our sanctification.

LEARNING OBJECTIVES

1. To grow in an understanding of the necessity of analogical language.
2. To become familiar with the historical underpinnings of the modern attacks on language via logical positivism.

QUOTATIONS AND THOUGHTS

God does not expect us to submit our faith to Him without reason, but the very limits of reason make faith a necessity. (Augustine)

Education without religion, as useful as it is, seems rather to make man a more clever devil. (C.S. Lewis)

LECTURE OUTLINE

I. The fourth principle that non-theists attack is the analogical use of language. The first three are the law of non-contradiction, causality, and the basic reliability of sense perceptions.

II. The God-Talk Controversy or Theothanatology
   a. In the late sixties, philosophers and theologians announced the death of God. The crisis came from the philosophy of logical positivism.
      i. The Law of Verification
      ii. "Only statements that can be verified empirically can be stated as true."
      iii. Illustration: Gold in Alaska
      iv. Analogical Use of Language
   b. The law of verification can't be verified empirically. Thus ended this school of thought. But its assertions remain and should be challenged.

III. Some Christians take pride in the inability of non-theists to disprove their experiences or personal faith in God.
   a. But ideas that cannot be disproved can also not be proved. This is "cheating." Illustration: Ghosts
   b. It is always easier to prove something than to disprove it. Illustration: Gold in Alaska Again
   c. Within formal logic (such as the law of non-contradiction), it is not difficult to disprove a point.

IV. How does logical positivism impact us today? And from whence did it come?
   a. Statements about God, according to the logical positivists, are merely emotive. Illustration: College Student and Significant Hymns
   b. What is behind such a pessimistic approach to God? 19th- and 20th- century redefinitions of historic Christianity into naturalistic terms.
   c. These naturalistic philosophers no longer needed God in their system because they suggested spontaneous generation as the means of creation of the universe.
   d. This also entailed a rejection of the supernatural.
   e. The theology that prevailed was pantheistic—God exists as part of the universe. This inability to speak about God as separate from His creation provoked the controversy that led to an overreaction—God is wholly other.
   f. Rather than being one with nature, God is totally above and beyond nature. This idea salvages God's transcendence, but ruins our ability to know God.

STUDY QUESTIONS

1. How and why did theologians and philosophers say that God "died"?

2. What is the difference between discussing your feelings about the existence of God and discussing whether God objectively exists?

3. After the Enlightenment of the 18th century, what philosophical movement followed that attacked the supernatural?

DISCUSSION QUESTIONS

1. If there is no connection between nature (including man) and God, we cannot draw analogies between God and man. What is the opposite problem that remains in our culture today? How can we respond biblically to both these assertions?

2. How does the general rejection of the supernatural affect your life, your church, or the Christian church as a whole?

9

Analogical Language (Part 2)

MESSAGE INTRODUCTION

God is holy. But He is not wholly other. There are similarities between us and God: those initiated as we were created with the "image of God" internally imprinted on us, and highlighted in the Incarnation, as God proved that He was not completely different from us by becoming a man. And when we reach heaven, "We shall be like Him, for we shall see Him as He is."

LEARNING OBJECTIVES

1. To understand the dangers of Karl Barth's idea of God as "wholly other."
2. To realize that the problems of communication can be overcome.
3. To understand the three kinds of language.

QUOTATIONS AND THOUGHTS

The incarnation of Christ is the clearest affirmation of the truth that man is created in the image of God. (Lawrence Adams)

Christ voluntarily took on himself everything that is inseparable from human nature. (John Calvin)

With the exception of being sinful, everything that can be said about a man can be said about Jesus Christ. (James Boice)

LECTURE OUTLINE

I. The Crisis of God-Talk and Karl Barth

Analogical Language (Part 2)

   a. Barth introduced the idea that God was wholly other to guard Him from being discussed rationally.
   b. Illustration: R.C. in Canada
   c. Illustration: *Cool Hand Luke* and a failure to communicate

II. Why do we fail to communicate?
   a. Illustration: I say "chair" and you hear "chair", and example of communication working.
   b. Illustration: I say "imminence" and you hear "M&M's."
   c. If you cannot understand language, you cannot know much. If language cannot communicate, then we can know nothing about God.

III. Aquinas and Three Kinds of Language
   a. Univocal: In a dialogue, when two parties understand a thing in exactly the same way. In this language, words retain their definitions.
   b. Equivocal: When, within a dialogue, the definitions of portion of the language changes meaning. When one person communicates something to the other, the meaning changes.
   c. Analogical: In communication, the definitions of words change proportionately to the difference in the beings dialoguing. Illustration: Good dog vs. Good guy
   d. We have a measured likeness to God; therefore, we have a corresponding ability to communicate with Him.

STUDY QUESTIONS

1. Who introduced the concept of God as "wholly other" into 20th-century theology?

2. According to Aquinas, what are the three kinds of communication? Give exaples of each in a conversation.

3. How does God's idea of goodness differ from ours?

DISCUSSION QUESTIONS

1. How does God's idea of love differ from ours? Of hate?

2. Have you ever tried to communicate with someone who was from a very different culture or situation from yours? Were you able to communicate?

3. Do the challenges of language help explain the reasons behind the Incarnation? Does this understanding of language show the importance of Jesus as the "Word made flesh"?

10

Contradiction and Paradox

MESSAGE INTRODUCTION

The law of contradiction is an important tool as we discover the difference between true but appropriately gray and murky ideas and truly incorrect ones. Some people are far too quick to assert that there are contradictions in the Christian faith. By making proper distinctions, however, it can be shown that there are none. If there are, then we should most certainly sleep in on Sundays.

LEARNING OBJECTIVES

1. To be able to distinguish between contradiction, paradox, and antinomy.
2. To be able to recognize and avoid religious-sounding reasons for being irrational.
3. To recognize that words change in their meaning with use and misuse.

QUOTATIONS AND THOUGHTS

Truth is not the feeble thing that men often think they can afford to disparage. Truth is power; let it be treated and trusted as such. (Horatius Bonar)

Truth is incontrovertible. Panic may resent it; ignorance may deride it; malice may distort it; but there it is. (Winston Churchill)

Truth is like our first parents—most beautiful when naked. (John Trapp)

Truth is sometimes daunting, but always worth knowing. (Thomas Winning)

LECTURE OUTLINE

I. Introduction to Contradiction, paradox, Antinomy, and Mystery
    a. Definitions and the Law of Contradiction

      b. Illustration: A doctor of philosophy
      c. Illustration: A German doctor of theology
      d. Illustration: Paul Tillich and the Ground of Being

II. Christian theology has no contradictions, but has paradoxes.
      a. Does God violate the law of non-contradiction?
      b. Though various theologians say that He does, using the Trinity as an example, no contradiction exists there. A paradox does.
      c. Gnostic and Jewish ideas about God were at variance in the early church.

III. Antinomy and Contradiction and Dr. Packer
      a. Dr. Packer uses a more British meaning for the term "antinomy." [Editor's Note: The three books mentioned by R.C. are titled *Evangelism and the Sovereignty of God*, *Knowing God*, and *Fundamentalism and the Word of God*. All three are by J. I. Packer.]
      b. In classic philosophy, antinomy and contradiction are synonyms.
      c. The confusion as to their definition occurs because they are rooted in different languages. "Contradiction" is rooted in Latin, while "antinomy" is rooted in Greek.

STUDY QUESTIONS

1. What is the difference between contradiction, paradox, and mystery?

2. Are there contradictions in the Christian faith? Why not?

DISCUSSION QUESTIONS

1. What are some words that have changed in definition in your time? Have any of these changes affected the expression of your faith?

2. How do you explain the Trinity to someone who says that it is a contradiction? How do you explain the Incarnation to someone who says that it is a contradiction?

3. What is your tendency: to call things "mysteries" just because you can't understand them, or to overanalyze the unknowable and try to make all the Christian faith fit into a set of propositions?

4. God has chosen to speak clearly about some things (the Gospel) and unclearly (although truthfully) about other things (the return of Christ). What instruction does this offer the church on how dogmatic to be on certain topics?

11

Mystery

MESSAGE INTRODUCTION

It appears as if few people have a biblical understanding of mystery. We tend to either see far too much mystery in the Bible, using it as an excuse to not think tough-mindedly about the Christian faith, or err by making our speculations about the obviously unclear into dogma. Let us strive to find the balance between holy awe and holy certitude.

LEARNING OBJECTIVES

1. To be able to accurately define "contradiction," "paradox," "antinomy" and "mystery."
2. To develop a confidence in God's essential rationality.
3. To see why the Christian faith is without contradiction.

QUOTATIONS AND THOUGHTS

Mysteria fidei: Mysteries of the faith. Doctrines known by revelation that transcend the grasp of reason or general revelation.

Mystery is but another name for our ignorance; if we were omniscient, all would be plain. (Tryon Edwards)

A religion without mystery is a religion without God. (Anon.)

Mystery is beyond human reason, but it is not against human reason. (Os Guiness)

LECTURE OUTLINE

I. Continuing: Contradiction, Paradox, Antinomy, and Mystery

Mystery

a. Recent editions of dictionaries muddy the waters even more.
b. Language is fluid, changing daily.
c. Etymology also plays a part in the definitions of words.
d. The Oxford English Dictionary (OED) shows us that words also have different usages at different times.
e. Words are also defined by modern usage. Formerly incorrect use can become correct, such as the term "ain't."

II. Christian theology has no contradictions
   a. Does God violate the law of non-contradiction?
   b. If Christianity contains contradictions, so does God.
   c. If God uses a higher "logic" than we do, one that allows Him to resolve contradictions in religion that we cannot, then we should not trust a single word of the Bible, for it could mean the very opposite in His higher "logic."

III. Mystery
   a. The Incarnation and the Trinity are both holy mysteries; God has hidden the exact way in which they are worked out.
   b. The finite cannot grasp the infinite.
   c. The mysterious nature of something does not mean that it does not exist. And it does not mean that we cannot penetrate the veil to some extent.
   d. Illustration: Electricity
   e. Mysterion is most often used by the Apostle John. To him, it is something that was hidden, but is now revealed.
   f. How does mystery relate to contradiction?
      i. both have unintelligibility, or a present lack of understanding, in common.
      ii. Both can be talked about intelligently, using inductive and deductive logic.
      iii. Additional information does not unravel true contradiction.

STUDY QUESTIONS

1. What consequences does Dr. Sproul report if you believe that God has a different kind of logic from ours?

2. What year was the council of Chalcedon finished? In discussing the nature of Christ, the council of Chalcedon used four _____ .

3. Will we have complete knowledge in heaven? Why not?

4. How does a mystery differ from a contradiction?

DISCUSSION QUESTIONS

1. Name three mysteries of the Christian faith. Should we study such matters and attempt to resolve them, or should we just appreciate them and not attempt to plumb their depths?

2. Read Deuteronomy 29:29. How does this passage apply to the study of mystery?

3. What aspect of the Christian faith gave you the most trouble prior to conversion? How was it cleared up? Are there any other areas of the Christian faith that puzzle you? Have you given up trying to understand them, are you treating them as unanswerable mysteries, or are you just trying to ignore them?

12

Natural Theology (Part 1)

MESSAGE INTRODUCTION

The heavens declare the glory of God, and they do so perfectly, lest natural man be able to say to God on Judgment Day, "You were not clear to me about Your commands!" God is clear, and for His glory, He is revealed through everything that is. This is a tool in our apologetical tool-belt that we must allow no one to take away.

LEARNING OBJECTIVES

1. To understand the terminology surrounding natural revelation.
2. To become familiar with the individuals who have taught on this topic.
3. To be able to answer the question, "What happens to the innocent native in Africa when he dies?"

QUOTATIONS AND THOUGHTS

That which a man spits against heaven shall fall back on his own face. (Thomas Adams)

Those that love darkness rather than light shall have their doom accordingly. (Matthew Henry)

The punishment of the sinner is not an arbitrary vengeance, but the due process of moral providence. (J.A. Motyer)

LECTURE OUTLINE

34 — Defending Your Faith

I. A new direction in our study begins with the principle of natural theology.
   a. The idea of natural theology has been assaulted in the 20th century.
   b. The name associated with natural theology is Thomas Aquinas. St. Augustine had developed ideas before him, St. Paul before him.

II. Natural theology flows from general revelation.
   a. Natural theology is a knowledge of God gained from nature. It is based on general revelation.
   b. General revelation is something God does; natural theology is something we develop.
      i. Special revelation is given through Scripture.
      ii. General revelation is given by God concerning Himself to every person and its content is limited. Perfectly true, but limited (Romans 1:18-20).
      iii. Mediate general revelation is given to all people through some medium; it is indirect; for example, "The heavens declare the glory of God."
      iv. Immediate general revelation is given directly (without a medium); by example, the innate sense of God and morality in every human soul. This is what Calvin called the *Sensus Divinitatus*.
   c. Why was it necessary for Christ to come? Because all are guilty. Romans 1:18-23 begins, "For the wrath of God is revealed from heaven against all ungodliness and unrighteousness of men, who suppress the truth in unrighteousness." *[margin: primary sin of all humanity / suppression of truth]*
   d. Natural theology is the foundation for God's righteous judgment of the world.

III. Was St. Aquinas saying that man, with unaided reason, has the intellectual capacity to know God? No. Both Aquinas and Augustine denied this, but affirmed that God divinely and perfectly reveals Himself in nature.

STUDY QUESTIONS

1. Define natural, general, and special revelation. *[handwritten: Natural — the knowledge of God that every human being has / general — mediate, immediate / special — Scripture. revelation of God through nature.]*

2. Does the Bible teach that God reveals Himself in nature? Please cite this passage and summarize its content. *[handwritten: Yes. Genesis]*

3. What happens to the poor innocent native in Africa who dies? Does he go to hell or heaven? *[handwritten: Those who hear the truth & suppress the truth]*

DISCUSSION QUESTIONS

[handwritten at bottom: Because although]

Natural Theology (Part 1)

1. Pick an object, such as a tree. Discuss what we can learn about its Creator as we observe it from one mile, in context of other trees and objects. Then zoom in to one foot away. Then take a microscope and explain what you learn about God from that angle. How does a tree manifest the glory of God on a variety of levels?

2. How does sin affect the way we understand general revelation?

3. Looking at Romans 1-2 and Ephesians 1-2, discuss why God is just to send the non-elect to eternal punishment.

Handwritten notes:

God → (rays shining down) → MAN

Revelation
A divine relevation in nature
↓
natural theology

St. Thomas Aquinas, Romans 1
Augustine, general revelat.

13

Natural Theology (Part 2)

MESSAGE INTRODUCTION

Some ideas are silly, and they go away as quickly as they came. Even the devil's best hacks can't make them respectable. But some ideas are more potent, and their evil must be taken more seriously. The idea of "double truth" that will be discussed today has been in existence for almost 1500 years and is enjoying a revival today. Give serious attention to it, for it has a power that withstands even the most careful critique. R.C. thinks it could even be alive in your heart.

LEARNING OBJECTIVES

1. To see the implications of the perceived relationship between nature and grace.
2. To understand the difference between distinction and separation.
3. To be alerted to the danger of the virulent idea of "double truth."

QUOTATIONS AND THOUGHTS

Duplex Veritas: Double Truth; the theory that an idea or fact can be true in one field of study, but false in another.

Islam: Founded by Muhammad (570—632). Its fundamental confession is, "There is no god but God and Muhammad is His prophet."

LECTURE OUTLINE

I. Natural Theology Defended

Natural Theology (Part 2)

    a. Francis Schaeffer was one who assessed Aquinas negatively by asserting that he separated nature and grace. While Schaeffer is much appreciated, in this we must disagree.

    b. Aquinas actually demonstrated nature and grace's unity of source.

II. What problem was Aquinas trying to solve?
   a. The greatest threat to the church during his time was Islam.
   b. Rather than progressing through evangelism or sword, Islam was advancing by philosophy. Averroes (1126–1198) and Avicenna (980–1037) were seeking a synthesis between Aristotle and Islamic-based philosophy.
   c. The "double truth" theory taught that something could be simultaneously true in philosophy and false in religion. Unfortunately, this concept transfers easily to the philosophies of our day.
   d. Many Christians and non-Christians embrace this philosophy when it is convenient. We call it "relativism."
   e. Aquinas distinguished between reason and faith, nature and grace, in order to deal with this relativistic philosophical challenge. There are certain things we can learn from natural theology that we do not learn from special revelation.
   f. Illustration: Molecular Biology
   g. There are *articulus mixtus,* or mixed articles, that can be learned from either source. For instance, the bare existence of God may be derived from both.

III. How do science and theology relate to one another?
   a. God has already displayed Himself through natural revelation.
   b. Genesis 1:1 does not end our search for proofs of God's existence in nature. It assumes that the search has already occurred.
   c. We see conflict between the Bible and science, between natural and supernatural revelation. In an ideal world, these conflicts would never arise.
   d. Copernicus was opposed by Roman Catholics and Reformers. And he corrected both with his discovery that the earth was not the center of the solar system. But he did not correct the Bible.
   e. God's revelation in nature is just as perfect as in Scripture.

STUDY QUESTIONS

1. In what way does Dr. Sproul disagree with Dr. Schaeffer on nature and grace? Why?

2. According to Dr. Sproul, how do science and theology relate?

DISCUSSION QUESTIONS

1. How do you see the "double truth" theory at work today? How does it work in your heart?

2. What are other examples of scientific information and theological beliefs quarreling? Discuss how theology and science should interact about human cloning?

14

Aquinas vs. Kant

MESSAGE INTRODUCTION

A "Pyrrhic victory" is a battle that was won, but at too great a cost. As the dust of history has settled, it is clear that Immanuel Kant won the mind of philosophy, appearing to destroy all arguments for the existence of God postulated by Aquinas that had held sway for hundreds of years. But at what cost? And did he truly win, or just appear to do so?

LEARNING OBJECTIVES

1. To review the debate between Aquinas and the theory of "Double Truth."
2. To be introduced to the four arguments for the existence of God used by Thomas Aquinas.
3. To understand the clash between Aquinas and Kant and the resulting irrationality from Kant's "victory."

QUOTATIONS AND THOUGHTS

He who leaves God out of his reasoning does not know how to count. (Anon.)

I could prove God statistically; take the human body alone—the chance that all the functions of the individual would just happen is a statistical monstrosity. (George Gallup)

If God did not exist, it would be necessary to invent him. (Voltaire)

LECTURE OUTLINE

I. Introduction: Thomas Aquinas and Natural Theology
   a. Aquinas was responding to the Muslim "double truth" theory.

b. Aquinas made potent arguments from philosophy and theology.
   c. We cooperate with the Holy Spirit in the proclamation and defense of Christianity.

II. Arguments for the Existence of God
   a. Ontological: Set forth by St. Anselm (1033-1109), based on God's nature
   b. Cosmological: Directly based on law of causality
   c. Teleological: From telos, and argument from design
   d. Moral: Based on uniform morality worldwide
   e. In all these, Aquinas synthesized philosophy (Aristotle) and theology. His arguments held sway until the publication of Immanuel Kant's *Critique of Pure Reason*, published around the time of the U.S. Revolution.

III. Kant's Rescue of Science
   a. Kant attempted to defeat pure reason and thereby make room for the existence of faith in religion.
   b. The noumenal and the phenomenal are Kant's two divisions of reality.
      i. Kant said that we cannot measure the noumenal world, but he offered that God, Self, and Essences existed there.
      ii. The phenomenal realm is the place we live—it is the world of appearances. It can be measured and observed.
      iii. Through the use of reason, we cannot get the phenomenal to the noumenal.
      iv. Kant said that for practical purposes, we must live as if there is a God in heaven. Meaningful ethics are impossible without an objective standard of virtue.
   c. Fideism was the result of this critique. It involves a "leap of faith" because rational proofs of God are abandoned.

IV. Kant and the New Testament
   a. Romans 1 says that God is known through general revelation. But if Kant is right, then the unbeliever has an excuse.
   b. If Paul is right, then Kant is wrong.
   c. Kant said that all arguments for God are based on the Ontological argument.
   d. St. Anselm said, "God is the greatest conceivable being. That greatest being cannot be merely a construct of the mind—He must have being or existence in order to be perfect. Therefore: God exists because He must exist."
   e. Kant countered by saying that existence is not an attribute.
   f. In Kant's system, reason may demand that God exists, but reality may not be rational. Thus, relativism and irrationality naturally flow from Kant's thesis.

STUDY QUESTIONS

1. What are the four arguments for God's existence made by Aquinas?

2. How did Kant critique Aquinas' rational arguments for God's existence?

3. How does the New Testament confirm or deny Kant's theories?

DISCUSSION QUESTIONS

1. As you think through the four arguments for God's existence, which one is most convincing to you? Why? Or do you think arguments for God's existence are a waste of time? Why?

2. Are there any other arguments for the existence of God distinct from these four? Explain, and offer any critique or approval possible.

handwritten at top: ① Membership Sunday / Sunday night / Wednesday

15

The Case for God

MESSAGE INTRODUCTION

What is the best way to explain the existence of God to a non-Christian? Is there one "best" way? The philosophical rubble from Kant's Pyrrhic victory over Aquinas has left Christians split over how apologetics should proceed. In this lecture, R.C. discusses the various options and identifies himself as a classical apologeticist.

LEARNING OBJECTIVES

1. To demonstrate the impact of Kantianism on modern apologetics.
2. To discuss the differences between evidentialist, classical, and presuppositional apologetics.
3. To demonstrate that logically, one must start with oneself in the quest to understand God's existence.

QUOTATIONS AND THOUGHTS

God is more truly imagined than expressed, and He exists more truly than is imagined. (Augustine)

We trust not because "a" god exists, but because "this" God exists. (C.S. Lewis)

Men and women who refuse to acknowledge God's existence do so, in the final analysis, because it is contrary to their manner of living. (R.C. Sproul)

LECTURE OUTLINE

I. The results of Kant's critique of the arguments for the existence of God were:
  a. The church was confused.
  b. Individuals were fideistic.

c. Illustration: Is there anyone else up there who can help me?
   d. "I believe Christianity because it is absurd."
   e. Empirical appeals to history and moral certitude (evidentialists). Note: R.C. is not an evidentialist, but is classical. This view holds that there is not merely a high degree of likelihood that God exists, but compelling proof.

II. Presuppositionalism: Another Reformed view of apologetics
   a. The book *Classical Apologetics* contains a critique of this viewpoint
   b. Dr. Cornelius VanTil, who taught at Westminster Theological Seminary, was native Dutch, and this is one reason why there are so many interpretations of his work.
   c. Presuppositionalism: In order to arrive at the conclusion that God exists, one must start with the premise that God exists. Without a foundation for reason, there can be no reason.
      i. Objection: This is a classic fallacy of circular reasoning. The conclusion appears in the premise.
      ii. Response: All reasoning moves in a circular fashion. Its start, middle and end relate to each other in a sense.
      iii. Objection: This is the fallacy of equivocation. Circular reasoning has been redefined in midstream.
      iv. Response: Greg Bahsen clarifies by saying that VanTil was saying that to assume rationality is in fact irrational without God's existence. You must assume the ground of reasoning before you affirm reason itself.
      v. Second main objection: Nobody starts with God unless you are God. Self-consciousness is where we start, not God-awareness.
      vi. Response: You are capitulating to secular ideas, specifically Enlightenment ideas.
      vii. Objection: This is not a deification of self, but self-consciousness. Augustine said that as soon as one knows that one exists, then you can know that you are not God. This ends in humility, not autonomy.
      viii. Presuppositionalists and classicists think the other is giving too much away to the world. Both agree that the construction of the idea of God is critical to the Christian life.

STUDY QUESTIONS

1. What are the differences between evidentialists, classicists, and presuppositionalists?

2. Why does R.C. teach that apologetics must start with acknowledgment that people exist?

DISCUSSION QUESTIONS

1. How do worldly ideas impact your apologetics and evangelism?

2. Write a dialogue between a Christian and non-Christian about God's existence. Was your dialogue more evidential, classical, or presuppositional?

16

Four Possibilities

MESSAGE INTRODUCTION

Many believe that what someone thinks about religion is his or her personal opinion, nothing more. Today, ideas about God are viewed as ultimately subjective, with no evidence supporting them, only bare feelings, intuition, or experience. In this study, Dr. Sproul makes it clear that not only are there reasons for God's existence, but if put together in a Biblical and logical fashion, there is proof for God's existence.

LEARNING OBJECTIVES

1. To be introduced to a means of proving the existence of God.
2. To gain confidence in doing apologetics.
3. To review the four possibilities that may explain reality.

QUOTATIONS AND THOUGHTS

Logic is the study of argument. As used in this sense, the word "argument" means not a quarrel (as when we "get into an argument"), but a piece of reasoning in which one or more statements are offered as support for some other statement. The statement being supported is the conclusion of the argument. The reasons given in support of the conclusion are called premises. We may say, "This is so and so (premises), therefore that is so (conclusion)." Premises are generally preceded by such words as because, for, since, on the ground that, and the like. Conclusions, on the other hand, are generally preceded by such words as therefore, hence, consequently, and it follows that. (S. Morris Engel)

LECTURE OUTLINE

I. There are several methods of establishing the existence of God.

II. Classical Apologetics: The First Steps

a. This method is influenced greatly by St. Augustine, who tried to establish a sufficient reason for the existence of God. This is done through a process of logical elimination.
b. We start with four possibilities to explain reality.
    i. *Illusion*: Reality is not real.
    ii. *Self-Created*: Reality came into existence through itself.
    iii. *Self-Existent*: Reality exists by its very nature.
    iv. *Created*: Reality is created by a self-existent being.
c. The simplest argument for the existence of God is, "If anything exists, God exists." That is, if something anywhere exists, then somewhere, there must be a self-existent being to make that so.
d. Illustration: Is the chalk here or not? How do we give sufficient evidence for this?
e. The first option is rarely held. The second option is the most popular option. The third option is rarely held, but more so than the first.
f. Reason demands the existence of some kind of self-existence.
g. The classical argument attempts to go beyond mere probability to proof. This will be a rational proof that compels a rational person to surrender to a rational proof.

III. Proof versus Persuasion
   a. Proof is objective.
   b. Persuasion is subjective.
   c. Illustration: Charlie is dead.

IV. Not a Neutral Question
   a. Unbelievers have an enormous vested interest to deny, deny, deny.
   b. We are not called to persuade people, but to give good reasons for God's existence.

STUDY QUESTIONS

1. What are the four ways to explain the nature of reality? Have you heard any ways that loosely fit into one of these categories?

2. What is the difference between proof and persuasion? To which is the Christian called?

3. The reason that people do not admit to God's existence is not so much a biblical or rational one as a _____ one.

DISCUSSION QUESTIONS

1. In your experience, what is the most popular option of the four explanations of reality? If you have ever discussed this topic with an unbeliever, recount that experience through writing it down or discussing it. What would you do differently?

2. People want to be free from guilt and accountability. If someone honestly states that this is his or her reason for not being a Christian or denying God's existence, how would you respond?

17

The Illusion of Descartes

MESSAGE INTRODUCTION

Rene' Descartes was a French philosopher and mathematician, born in La Haye, France. In Bavaria, in the winter of 1619, he took on the mission to re-create the philosophical world by doubting every assumption and building a philosophy based on math. It may seem as though he was a wild-eyed mystic, but he was actually very quiet and careful, keeping many of his books from publication because Roman Catholicism was in the very act of condemning Galileo's work. But after his works were released, they caused a storm in philosophy and apologetics that still troubles and amazes us.

LEARNING OBJECTIVES

1. To begin a critique of the four explanations of reality.
2. To discuss the philosophy of Descartes and its impact on apologetics.

QUOTATIONS AND THOUGHS

I can only trace the lines that flow from God. (Albert Einstein)

Sin has gotten man into more trouble than science can get him out of. (Vance Havner)

The scientific way of looking at the world is not wrong any more than the glassmaker's way of looking at the window. This way of looking at things has its very important uses. Nevertheless the window was placed there not to be looked at, but to be looked through; and the world has failed of its purpose unless it too is looked through and the eye rests not on it, but on its God. (B.B. Warfield)

LECTURE OUTLINE

I. We start with four possibilities to explain reality.

The Illusion of Descartes

   a. *Illusion*: Reality is not real.
   b. *Self-Created*: Reality came into existence through itself.
   c. *Self-Existent*: Reality exists by its very nature.
   d. *Created*: Reality is created by a self-existent being.

II. Descartes' Critique of Reality as Illusion
   a. Rene' Descartes (1596-1650), a mathematician, was confronted by a wave of irrationality, an epistemological breakdown.
   b. The controversies of Copernicus and the Reformation and Galileo created a crisis of authority.
   c. Descartes attempted to restore certitude. "Clear and distinct ideas" were his goal, ideas that could reconstruct man's search for knowledge.
   d. Illustration: What are ten things that I know for sure?
   e. Descartes doubted everything that he could conceivably doubt, and whatever was left, that is where he would begin. Perhaps everything was just the dream of a demon, he offered.
   f. He found that the one thing he could not doubt was that he was doubting. There is no way to escape the reality of doubt and the underlying reality that there is a doubter.

III. Assumptions of Self-Consciousness: *Cogito, Ergo Sum*
   a. If Descartes is right, then whatever else is in doubt, our existence is not in doubt.
   b. Going a bit further, if a piece of chalk actually exists, then a self-existent Creator must exist.
   c. The two major assumptions of Descartes in this formula are the law of non-contradiction and the law of causality.

STUDY QUESTIONS

1. What events and people caused an upheaval in epistemology in the 16th and 17th centuries?

2. What are five things that you know for sure? Why?

3. Why is self-existence an argument for the existence of a Creator?

DISCUSSION QUESTIONS

1. There is a problem of authority in the Protestant church today. How does your church deal with this problem? Does Roman Catholicism solve the problem by claiming or functioning as a final authority?

2. When is the last time you dialogued with someone about the existence of God? Can you speak more often about such matters with your children, your workmates, people on the Internet?

18

Self-Creation (Part 1)

MESSAGE INTRODUCTION

As we understand how to defend the Christian faith, we are often caught off guard by the incredible faith displayed by our opponents in very bad ideas. It takes a tremendous exercise of faith to believe in self-creation theories, and as R.C. will point out in this lecture, the faith of the true believer is not enough to save a very bad idea from destroying itself. This idea's time has come and gone.

LEARNING OBJECTIVES

1. To review the possible alternatives to reality.
2. To critically review the alternative of self-creation.
3. To understand how important this idea is to many agnostic systems of thought.

QUOTATIONS AND THOUGHTS

Dear me, the Lord got on very well before I was born, and I'm sure He will when I am dead. (C.H. Spurgeon)

God is not in need of anything, but all things are in need of God. (Marcianus Aristides)

God is the cause of all causes, the soul of all souls. (A.H. Strong)

LECTURE OUTLINE

I. What possible alternatives are there to explain reality?

       a. Illusion
       b. Self-creation
       c. Self-existence
       d. Creation via self-existent being

II. Self-creation is the most frequent alternative offered to theists
    a. This is a generic principle that subsumes many generic principles and arguments.
    b. Self-creation is analytically false; it is false by definition. For something to be its own cause, it would have to preexist itself. It would be and not be at the same time and in the same relationship.

III. Past and Current Theories of Self-Creation
    a. French encyclopedists such as Denis Diderot (1713-1784) were determined anti-theists, and suggested spontaneous generation as the means of creation.
    b. The counter argument to this teaching is *ex nihilo, nihil fit*—out of nothing, nothing comes.
    c. In 1953, a Nobel Prize winner said that we should replace the idea of spontaneous generation with the concept of *gradual* spontaneous generation.
    d. The Hubble Telescope was launched on April 25, 1990. A famed physicist explained on that day that the beginnings of the universe occurred 15-20 billion years ago, when it exploded into "being." But this is more a philosophical statement than astrophysical one.
    e. "Creation by chance" is the most popular way we hear this taught today. Space + time + chance = stuff is the overly hopeful way in which this is formulated.

STUDY QUESTIONS

1. How does self-creation "fix" the problem of the existence of God for the non-Christian atheist?

2. Why is self-creation false by definition?

3. What misunderstandings of chance play a part in the theories of self-creation?

DISCUSSION QUESTIONS

1. What are other ways in which non-Christians attempt to solve the "God" problem by making Him unneeded?

2. How is some form of self-creation an important part of evolutionary thinking?

3. Some people create God or supernatural involvement because they need Him to fix their systems. But we know God exists to do more than fill gaps in our understanding. How is the theory of self-creation a "god of the gap" theory?

19

Self-Creation (Part 2)

MESSAGE INTRODUCTION

Have you ever thought about an idea so much that it made your head hurt? Concepts like eternity and the way the Trinity works and how God is thinking about you and sustaining you this very moment . . . these are ideas so large, they leave us mentally breathless before too long. Some ideas leave us breathless because they are so fundamentally wrong. The self-creation of the universe is one of those. Like a thousand-pound weight on the shoulders, not everything that strains human capacity is good exercise.

LEARNING OBJECTIVES

1. To critically consider the idea that the universe is self-created.
2. To analyze the common use of the word "chance."
3. To be able to show through illustration the irrationality of self-creation if ascribed to the universe.

QUOTATIONS AND THOUGHTS

When we think of anything that has origin, we are not thinking of God. God is self existent, while all created things necessarily originate somewhere at some time. (A.W. Tozer)

The wisdom of the flesh is always exclaiming against the mysteries of God. (John Calvin)

LECTURE OUTLINE

I. Creation by Chance: *Not a Chance*

a. Caveat: I am not a physicist. But the inferences that they draw from their data are often stated irrationally.
b. Arthur Koestler: "As long as chance rules, God is an anachronism." But it is necessary for chance only to exist for God to be destroyed; chance does not need to rule, only to exist, to eliminate God from our equations.

II. Physics by Illustration
   a. Illustration: A Quarter and a Harvard Professor
   b. Illustration: R.C., Al, and a Train

III. What is chance?
   a. Modern jargon has elevated the term "chance" beyond the definition of mathematical odds. It has been colloquially given some kind of power and ontology.
   b. Ontology is the study of being. Chance has no being. It is only conceptual.
   c. Chance is no-thing.
   d. Niels Bohr: *Contraria un Complementaria* or "Contrary Complementarity." Contradictions are complementary.
   e. Heisenberg's Principle of Uncertainty: We can't explain the behavior of some subatomic particles. But to move from this lack of explanation to inferring that nothing is producing the effect is irrational.
   f. Nonsense and bad science are the result of self-existence theories.

STUDY QUESTIONS

1. If chance exists, how does this destroy God?

2. How did R.C. show the Harvard professor that chance does not exist? Does this convince you? Why or why not?

3. Explain Heisenberg's principle or uncertainty. How is it true? How do some misuse it?

DISCUSSION QUESTIONS

1. The problem with modern physics is not scientists' experimentations, conclusions, or methods. The problem with many sciences is the irrational inferences from uncertain conclusions. What are some other unwarranted conclusions to which some modern atheists jump to undergird their ideas?

2. If chance is not a thing, then are numbers things? Is any idea a thing?

3. There is, from our perspective, chaos in this world. Why does it look so chaotic?

20

Self-Existence

MESSAGE INTRODUCTION

As we look at various options to explain reality, this one has a bit of truth to it. Something indeed is self-existent; it's just not the universe. The best arguments for the self-existent universe are often too strong—they end up suggesting that the universe is more than self-existent, that it is also self-aware. At that point, we chuckle and welcome them to our side. That's what Christians have believed all along.

LEARNING OBJECTIVES

1. To review and critique the argument for the self-existence of the universe.
2. To be able to show how the Bible assumes God's self-existence.
3. To be introduces to key phrases and words in this ancient discussion,

QUOTATIONS AND THOUGHTS

Philosophy is saying what everyone knows in language no one can understand. (J.F. Taviner)

Good philosophy must exist, for bad philosophy needs to be answered. (C.S. Lewis)

Aseitas: Latin. Aseity, self-existence, or *autotheos* (Greek).

LECTURE OUTLINE

I. Explaining Reality
    a. Illusion: Not an option
    b. Self-created: Irrational
    c. Self-existence: Something is self-existent, but not the universe
    d. Created by self-existent being: True

II. Self-Existent and Eternal: Rational or Not?
    a. Some philosophers have argued that if anything can be conceived of rationally, it must be real. This is rationality gone wild.
    b. Illustration: Unicorns and Ducks and Deer
    c. A self-existent being is not irrational. It is not contradictory to the law of causality, because a being is not an effect.
    d. But just because we can conceive of such a being does not mean that it exists. It is also rationally conceivable that nothing exists now or ever—obviously, that is not true.
    e. If something exists, the idea of the self-existent being becomes more than possible: it becomes necessary.

III. Self-Existence as Necessary (Aseity)
    a. Self-existent beings do not grow from anything.
    b. *Ens Necessarium*: That being whose being is necessary.
    c. If there was a time when there was absolutely nothing, then there would still be nothing because *ex nihilo, nihil fit*. We are arguing that there must be something that has the power of being and always has been, or nothing else (or nothing at all) could exist.
    d. Ontological Necessity: Ontology is the science of being. God exists by the necessity of His own being—by His very nature, He must exist, or else He is not God.
    e. Moses: "Who are you?" God: "I AM."

STUDY QUESTIONS

1. Why is self-existence not irrational?

2. What does the word "ontology" mean?

3. Translate *ex nihilo, nihil fit*: _____

DISCUSSION QUESTIONS

1. Explain why it is rationally necessary that something is self-existent in or outside the universe.

2. Put yourself back at the burning bush, in Moses' sandals. After you have read that text (Exodus 3), what can you say that Moses learned about God there? Anything new? Anything your culture needs to review?

21

Necessary Being

MESSAGE INTRODUCTION

General revelation and special revelation are both true. That which we can learn through a telescope is no less true than that which we learn from St. Paul. But while special revelation is settled in the Scriptures, general revelation is like a stream, forever changing as we scrape the surface of God's glory in creation. R.C. reports that current secular theories of surrounding creation are still woefully inadequate and suspiciously silent about the cause of their "Big Bang."

LEARNING OBJECTIVES

1. To be able to show the necessity of God's existence outside the universe, contra the immanentistic view.
2. To understand that philosophy and science have argued for the existence of a necessary power that has many qualities of the Christian God.

QUOTATIONS AND THOUGHTS

Logical Fallacy: Ad Hominem Abuse or Personal Attack. An argument that substitutes abusive remarks instead of evidence to prove their conclusion. An example would be, "Kim thinks homosexuals are going to hell, but she's just a know-it-all judgmental Jesus-freak. You can't believe her."

World Soul: A phrase used by pantheistic or New Age philosophers to explain that since the world creates and sustains life, it must have life itself, and a soul as other creatures. Also called panpsychism.

LECTURE OUTLINE

I. Explaining Reality
   a. Illusion: Not an option
   b. Self-created: Irrational
   c. Self-existence: Something is self-existent, but is it the universe?
   d. Created by self-existent being

II. The State of Nature
   a. The Big Bang theory (not accepted as recently as the 1940s) affirms that 15-18 billion years ago, something existed. A singularity, a compaction of all matter, existed. It grew unstable and exploded, creating the universe as we know it, a movement from organization to chaos.
   b. How did nature become organized in the first place?
   c. The law of inertia says that things in motion (or not in motion) tend to remain as they are unless acted on by an outside force. How did the universe move from rest to activity?
   d. Illustration: Golf in Motion
   e. What cause the Bang? It is necessary to answer this question, and highly unusual that science would plead that this is an unimportant question. Since when did causality become unimportant?
   f. Matter is mutable. It manifests contingency. Materialists will respond that the things we see are not immutable. They claim that the entity that makes matter is not transcendent, but immanent.
   g. Materialists say that whatever causes matter is part of the universe or is the sum total of the universe. Some force pulsates through all things that forms a self-existent core, and this accounts for the causality of the beginning of the universe.
   h. Thus: They argue that there is no need for a transcendent God. A self existent eternal power, yes. But not outside the universe.

III. The Answer to the Materialist Challenge
   a. If you mean by "universe" all that is (and God is), then it is true that God is inside the universe.
   c. But transcendence is not a geographical description. It is an ontological distinction. It says that God is a higher order of being, not that He is located elsewhere.
   d. If there is some unknown, immeasurable, eternal being that transcends everything that is derived from it, then our argument is mere semantics. The materialist has won, but won for which side?

IV. The Unmoved Mover and the God of the Bible: What is the connection? The next two lectures will demonstrate this.

STUDY QUESTIONS

1. Name the four ways by which one can explain reality.

2. What part of the Big Bang theory are scientists strangely silent on?

3. Define "transcendent" and explain why it is critical that God be so described.

DISCUSSION QUESTIONS

1. In pop-philosophy, New Age thinking reigns supreme. The New Agers' god is the earth, and they worship it as living, breathing, and cognitive. Have you ever discussed the existence of the Christian God with a New Ager? How did that conversation go? If you have not talked to one, write an imaginary dialogue, and confront him with the good news of a transcendent God that became immanent in Christ.

2. Is your god more like Aristotle's unmoved mover, or is he more active—perhaps too active?

22

God of the Bible vs. God of Philosophy

MESSAGE INTRODUCTION

Apologetics is often downplayed or downright ridiculed as arguing for a sub-Christian God. It must be admitted that general revelation can tell us much less about God than the Bible, but if it tells us truth, then we should press it upon men and women as a partial, but accurate, picture of the God they should worship. Dr. Sproul explains in this lecture how partial knowledge of God is not necessarily untrue.

LEARNING OBJECTIVES

1. To understand the effects of Greek culture on Christianity.
2. To be encouraged to use apologetics.
3. To be able to demonstrate that deism is an irrational stopping point in philosophical understandings of God.

QUOTATIONS AND THOUGHTS

Deus Absconditus/Deus Revelatus: Latin, "the hidden God/the revealed God." This is the paradox that God has revealed Himself in a way that defies the wisdom of this world because it is the revelation of a hidden God. This is foolishness to Greeks, a stumbling block to Jews, but salvation for those to whom God reveals Himself.

Deus Otiosus: Latin, "the idle God." This is an ancient name for deism and has been denied by every branch of the church. The God of the Bible is not silent or impotent.

LECTURE OUTLINE

I. Explaining Reality Revisited
   a. Illusion: Not an option
   b. Self-created: Irrational
   c. Self-existence: Something is self-existent, but is it the universe?
   d. Created by self-existent being

II. What does Athens have to do with Jerusalem?
   a. The church father Tertullian was famous for his distinction between the personal God of Israel and the vague, abstract concept or principle of Greek philosophy.
   b. This objection was raised afresh by Adolf von Harnack and Albrecht Ritschl, liberal theologians who questioned whether Christianity had been poisoned by Greek philosophy in its understanding of the nature of God.
   c. This charge remains in that many suspect that systematicians impose a philosophical system on the Bible and try to squeeze the Bible into it.
   d. But this charge presupposes that the Bible is in disarray and has no interior logical arrangement. We believe it does, and systematic theology seeks to discover and articulate it.

III. God used Greek and Hebrew.
   a. The Holy Spirit did use Greek language to communicate Jewish (Hebrew) ideas about God.
   b. There are sharp differences (though some similarities) between the god of Aristotle (the Unmoved Mover) and the God of the Bible.

IV. God as Incomprehensible
   a. We believe not that God is beyond knowing, but that we do not have a complete and exhaustive knowledge of Him.
   b. Must we have a complete knowledge of God to have true knowledge of God?
   c. The arguments made for the existence of God give us nowhere near the God as revealed in the Bible. But that does not mean that those arguments yield something that is not a true, partial picture of the true God.

V. How do you get from "god" to "God"?
   a. Illustration: Anthony Flew's Explorer in the Jungle
   b. His parable still does not account for the existence of the jungle.
   c. Enlightenment philosophers could not escape this problem; and thus they could retreat no further than deism. They could not account for the design, but they could keep God at a distance—impersonal.
   d. But an impersonal god is no god at all.

STUDY QUESTIONS

1. Did Tertullian reject or embrace the Greek concepts of God?

2. What objections concerning Greek influences were raised by liberal theologians of the 19th century?

3. Is partial knowledge about God false because it is limited?

DISCUSSION QUESTIONS

1. Partial knowledge about something can be wrong—but it need not be incorrect by its very nature. Name three things we know very little about, but believe to be true.

2. Name a system of interpretation or system of presuppositions that is imposed on the Bible that does violence to its meaning (such as Mormonism). How does the Bible critique those points of difference in this specific unbiblical system?

3. Why is an impersonal god useless and irrational? How personal is your God?

23

Kant's Moral Argument

MESSAGE INTRODUCTION

Kant believed he had destroyed the traditional arguments for the existence of God, but he realized that this was more than philosophy (and the world) could bear. Committing the logical fallacy of "Appeal to Consequences of Belief," he let the horrors of a world without God convince him to find another argument for God's existence. His famous argument was the moral argument for God's existence. R.C. will explain that argument today.

LEARNING OBJECTIVES

1. To understand why Kant made a moral argument for God's existence
2. To believe more deeply the scriptural teaching on conscience and judgment.

QUOTATIONS AND THOUGHTS

Many a man has enough conscience to scare him in sin, but not enough to save him from sin. (C.H. Spurgeon)

The torture of a bad conscience is the hell of a living soul. (John Calvin)

A guilty conscience needs no accuser. (Anon)

LECTURE OUTLINE

I. Kant's Proofs For and Against God
   a. He denied the four main arguments for the existence of God.
   b. But he recognized the importance of having a god. Using the moral argument, he summarized the need for a god.

II. The New Testament and Morality
   a. He denied the four main arguments for the existence of God.
   b. But he recognized the importance of having a god. Using the moral argument, he summarized the need for a god.

III. The New Testament and Morality
   a. Romans 1:28-32 discussed immoral behavior.
   b. Paul makes it clear that people sin against what they know is right.
   c. The law is written on our hearts—this is what we call a conscience. That faculty can be harmed, or almost destroyed, in the case of the sociopath.

IV. Why Humans Need God
   a. While Kant said that conscience is a universal sense of oughtness, our culture does almost everything it can to flee from it.
   b. Illustration: Lady Macbeth
   c. Kant said that guilt came from failing to do our duty.
   d. Kant did not know whether knowledge about God was possible, but if it were possible, what would it have to be? This is how he constructed this argument.
   e. Old Testament saints aked, "Why do the wicked prosper and the righteous suffer?" If we follow Kant's logic, since there is not perfect justice on this side of the grave, then there must be an afterlife, and in that afterlife, there must be justice and one to mediate rewards and punishment.
   f. Finally, the judge must be perfect, stronger than any counterforce.
   g. And if we believe this, said Kant, we have hope for civilization and community.

V. The Existentialist Response
   a. You have shrunk away from the awful truth—life is meaningless.
   b. Those who won't affirm God's existence live on borrowed capital; they do not want God, but they want some kind of morality.
   c. Kant knew that you could not have one without the other.

STUDY QUESTIONS

1. What drove Kant to make an argument for God's existence after he had apparently destroyed the four most famous ones?

2. What does Romans 1-2 teach about the conscience?

3. Kant believed that guilt came from _____.

DISCUSSION QUESTIONS

1. How are God's judgment of mankind and our conscience connected?

2. If God does not exist, is there any reason whatsoever to be moral? How would you answer someone who wanted it both ways—a moral world and a godless universe?

3. How careful are you to listen to your conscience? Look up the word "conscience" in your concordance or Bible software and do a word study. Is it ever wise to go against your conscience?

24

Vanity of Vanity

MESSAGE INTRODUCTION

Immanuel Kant recognized that for societal purposes, a moral god had to exist. He was chided for his sensibilities by the existentialists and nihilists, as they claimed the courage to face up to the facts: everything, including ethics, was meaningless. And according to the Book of Ecclesiastes, they were right. Life under the sun is futile, just a sunrise, a sunset, and nothing in between. R.C. explains in this lecture why the meaning of life is found somewhere outside it.

LEARNING OBJECTIVES

1. To understand the interaction between Kant and nihilists who followed him.
2. To be able to demonstrate the Biblical evidence for the nihilist's philosophy.
3. To consider whether Christianity is an escape from a hopeless reality.

QUOTATIONS AND THOUGHTS

Logical Fallacy: Appeal to Tradition. This is a fallacy of logic that occurs when someone claims that an idea is correct because it is older or traditional. This argument is fallacious because the age of something does not automatically make it correct or better than something newer. For instance: The theory that the world rides on the back of a giant turtle is much older than modern understanding of the orbit of the earth around the sun. Therefore, the world rides on the back of a turtle. Or: The early church fathers prayed to the saints. This idea is older than the Protestant Reformation, which taught that we should not. Therefore, all Christians should pray to the saints.

LECTURE OUTLINE

I. Kant believed that for society to be sustained, we needed a moral god.
   a. Not everyone agreed with him. Cynics rightly pointed out that this is just wishful thinking.
   b. Many different philosophical systems exist, but the ones that disagreed with Kant were on the far pole, full-bodied nihilists.

II. The Bible often speaks in terms of these two poles.
   a. Wisdom literature, such as Psalms, Proverbs, Job, and Ecclesiastes, discusses life from the perspective of the theist, who loves God's law, and the wicked, who care for no one and nothing.
   b. Ecclesiastes is most easily compared to Kant's categories.
      i. The "under the sun" concept could be Kant's phenomenal world, while the place where God lives would be the noumenal.
      ii. The writer of Ecclesiastes agrees with Kant that there is no meaning to life in the phenomenal world.
      iii. "Vanity of vanity" is a superlative expression, like "Holy, holy, holy," "Lord of lords," or "666."
      iv. Vanity is synonymous with futility or meaninglessness.

III. Few philosophers are willing to embrace a meaningless existence.
   a. Most find some ground in the middle, but as Francis Schaeffer said, they have their feet firmly planted in midair.
   b. Systems that live in this middle ground live on borrowed capital from Christianity to enable them to have any reasonability or value.
   c. Paul made it clear in 1 Corinthians 15 that without Christ's resurrection, Christianity is meaningless and we deserve to be pitied.
   d. Albert Camus came to the conclusion that without God, the only serious question left to man is how and when to commit suicide.
   e. Illustration: School's out, but only for a while.
   f. Jean-Paul Sartre's book Nausea spoke of man as a "useless passion."
   g. Nietzsche was committed to living a life of courage in the midst of meaninglessness. He was going to face up to the reality of the situation and not flee from it. No escapism through religion—only the hard truth.

IV. Escaping the Problem
   a. Some have embraced the futility of life, but then attempted to escape it by hedonism or some other pleasure-oriented means.
   b. Marx said that religion was the opium of the people.
   c. But while some may say that Christianity is a crutch, and it certainly is for some, the truth is that the philosophy surrounding and supporting atheism appears to serve the same function.

STUDY QUESTIONS

1. Why did Kant believe that we need, in spite of evidence to the contrary, a moral god?

2. What did existentialists offer to counter Kant's proposal?

3. How does the Bible affirm or deny the nihilistic worldview?

DISCUSSION QUESTIONS

1. Have you ever met a real nihilist who believed that all of life was futile? Were you one at one time? Explain any personal experiences you've had with nihilism.

2. How do many of the secular media outlets preach nihilism?

3. As we dialogue with those who claim to not value anything, we can point out their inconsistencies and prove that a real nihilist would have no reason to get out of bed in the morning. Looking at Scripture (especially Ecclesiastes), what should we say to those who believe that everything is vanity?

25

The Psychology of Atheism

MESSAGE INTRODUCTION

If there is not God, why are there theists? This question resounded down the halls of many 19th-century universities. The answer: "Psychological necessity." R.C. asks the atheists to look in the morror and turn the question around: "If there is a God, why are there atheists?" The answer will be discussed in this lecture, and is further discussed in R.C.'s book, *If There Is a God, Why Are There Athiests?*

LEARNING OBJECTIVES

1. To understand the factor of psychological need in various belief systems.
2. To recognize the obvious emotional baggage that goes into an active denial of the reality of God or veracity of Christianity
3. To be reminded that God is to be feared and that He is far too threatening and powerful to be used as an emotional bandage.

QUOTATIONS AND THOUGHTS

If sin is man's contradiction of God and his expressed will, God cannot be complacent about sin and still be God. (Saphir Athyal)

There is power in God to lay prostrate the whole world, and to tread it under His feet, whenever it may please Him. (John Calvin)

The wrath of God is not ignoble. Rather, it is too noble, too perfect—it is this that bothers us. (James Boice)

LECTURE OUTLINE

I. Moral Courage and Theism

- a. In the 19th century, atheists charged that all religion flowed from emotional need or weakness.
- b. R.C. wrote a book called *If There Is a God, Why Are There Atheists?* to answer this charge and turn it around on them.
- c. This debate between atheism and theism isn't a contest to see who is smartest. There are brilliant people on both sides. But those people have, to one degree or another, bias.
- d. Illustration: Only Two People Didn't Care
- e. With every fiber of being, I want God to exist. But this is proof neither for—or against—His reality.
- f. The emotional baggage that atheists bring to the God-question is not a proof that they are incorrect, either. But it is revealing, and it is explained in Scripture.

II. Romans 1 and the Psychology of Atheism
- a. Romans 1:28 says, "For the wrath of God is revealed from heaven against all ungodliness and unrighteousness of men." There are things in that verse that puzzle or frustrate Christians and non-Christians.
- b. God is not just wrathful, but furious.
    - i. Why is He angry?
    - ii. Why do we suppress knowledge of Him?
    - iii. How does this phenomenon translate to psychotherapeutic ideas, such as repression?
- c. The greatest fear of humanity is not a meaningless existence.
    - i. It is a holy God that never forgets.
    - ii. We are naked before Him, and this nakedness makes us want to flee.

STUDY QUESTIONS

1. What charge was leveled by 19th century atheists concerning religious people?

2. Does the reality of emotional baggage in religious belief verify or falsify that system of belief? Why or why not?

3. What is man's greatest fear?

DISCUSSION QUESTIONS

1. When you were converted, did it meet a specific felt need, such as removing guilt, removing a compulsive behavior, answering a stressful question? What does this prove? What does it not prove?

2. How much should Christians focus on God's wrath? Why is the God of popular reli-

gion so nice and tame, devoid of all anger?

3. Should Christians fear God? In what sense are we forbidden to fear, and in what sense are we commanded to?

26

The Bible and Apologetics (Part 1)

MESSAGE INTRODUCTION

How do we defend the Bible from the skeptics? And how do we then use the Bible in apologetics? The next five lectures from Dr. Sproul will:

- Establish a solid starting point for using the Bible (26)
- Establish its normative authority (27)
- Establish a noncircular principle of self-attestation (28)
- Discuss the doctrine of inspiration and address Barth's critique (29)
- Introduce us to John Calvin's teaching on the authority of Scripture (30)

LEARNING OBJECTIVES

1. To outline three reasons why a purely circular argument, "The Bible says it is God's Word; God's Word is always true; therefore, the Bible is God's Word," is not acceptable in apologetics.
2. To be able to discuss the function of miracles in apologetics.
3. To be able to demonstrate that the claims of the Bible about itself are important.

QUOTATIONS AND THOUGHTS

When you drink from the stream, remember the spring. (Anon.)

One proof of the inspiration of the Bible is that it has withstood so much poor preaching. (A.T. Robertson)

LECTURE OUTLINE

I. Is the beginning of apologetics the trustworthiness of Scripture?
    a. Some think this is a way to avoid so many laborious arguments about the deity of Christ and the other truth claims of the Bible.
    b. But that is not the place to start. You don't know that the Bible is the Word of God if you don't know that there is a God.

II. There are others who argue that no rational defense should be given to the Bible or God.
    a. If we try to prove the Bible or God, some say, we are subjecting them to a higher authority (whatever you are using to prove them), and the Bible and God have intrinsic authority.
    b. But these kinds of arguments leave us with only circularity at the beginning of our apologetic.

III. Why is a circular argument to be avoided in apologetics?
    a. It is obviously fallacious. Any pagan can object to your entire apologetic on the basis of the logical fallacy of begging the question or petitio principii.
    b. The Bible is not the only book to claim to be the true expression of God's will. The Koran does this as well, as do the various documents associated with Mormonism. So we need other criteria to distinguish among these "divine" books.
    c. God offers proofs and authentications for His Word throughout redemptive history through miracles. He does not seem to think external authentication is denigrating to the Bible or His Being.

IV. Hume's Objections to Supernaturalism
    a. Some disapprove of the Bible precisely because it claims validation via the miraculous.
    b. Naturalistic assumptions turn the "proof" into a liability.

V. Where do we start with the Bible?
    a. Wherever we start, the internal claims that the Bible makes cannot be ignored.
    b. They make the job of arguing for the veracity of the Scriptures more difficult, raising the stakes higher. It's not just a good book, not just true, but inspired. Our apologetic for the Bible must take into account its claims about itself.

The Bible and Apologetics (Part 1)

STUDY QUESTIONS

1. Why is a circular argument for the Bible not helpful?

2. Why are the miracles in the Bible both helpful and a complicating factor in developing an apologetic for the truth of the Scriptures?

3. What impact on apologetics is made by the Bible's claims about itself?

DISCUSSION QUESTIONS

1. Since every idea starts with God and ends with God, in one sense, every argument is circular. How can we distinguish between bad circular arguments like the ones Dr. Sproul has illustrated and all other broadly circular arguments?

2. Have you experienced something that validates the claims of the Bible? Explain. How can this experience be used in your apologetics?

3. Most faith healers claim that God has given them the power to heal and that therefore, this validates everything that they have to say about the Bible. In what sense are they right? In what sense are they wrong?

27

The Bible and Apologetics (Part 2)

MESSAGE INTRODUCTION

How do we defend the Bible from the skeptics? And how do we then use the Bible in apologetics? In the second of five lectures from Dr. Sproul, he will:

- Establish a solid starting point for using the Bible (26)
- **Establish its normative authority (27)**
- Establish a noncircular principle of self-attestation (28)
- Discuss the doctrine of inspiration and address Barth's critique (29)
- Introduce us to John Calvin's teaching on the authority of scripture (30)

LEARNING OBJECTIVES

1. To be able to show the role of miracles in establishing authority.
2. To be able to discuss the practical implications of the authority of the Bible.
3. To be reminded that the Bible claims to have its source in God.

QUOTATIONS AND THOUGHTS

The word of the Lord is a light to guide you, a counselor to counsel you, a comforter to comfort you, a staff to support you, a sword to defend you, and a physician to cure you. The Word is a mine to enrich you, a robe to clothe you, and a crown to crown you. (Thomas Brooks)

Philosophy and religion may reform, but only the Bible can transform. (Brian Edwards)

A single line in the Bible has consoled me more than all the books I have ever read. (Immanuel Kant)

The Bible and Apologetics (Part 2)

LECTURE OUTLINE

I. Naturalism's Influences
   a. The Bible claims to have a supernatural origin and claims supernatural validation along the way of redemptive history.
   b. If God does speak in Scripture, then that fact ends a great many of the pointless discussions in our culture.

II. Practical Authority of the Bible
   a. This is not just an ivory-tower discussion.
   b. Illustration: R.C. the Counselor
   c. The Bible's authority is not questioned only in the university, but also in the church.

III. The Claims of the New Testament Writers
   a. In 2 Timothy 3, Paul claimed personal authority distinct from the authority of the Bible. The Bible stood on its own.
   b. Paul makes a universal affirmative when discussing the Bible (3:16).
   c. B.B. Warfield reminds us that the Bible is literally "God-breathed." Ultimately, the Bible is not based on Paul or Peter or the church, but God.
   d. In a sense, the Bible's authority is better explained by the term "expiration."
   e. The apostles accepted the Bible's claims about itself and built on those claims as they pressed God's truth upon those around them.

STUDY QUESTIONS

1. What is the role of the miracle in establishing the authority of the Bible?

2. How have legitimate Biblical studies disintegrated into "Biblical vandalism"?

3. Did the New Testament writers claim to be speaking by the authority of God?

DISCUSSION QUESTIONS

1. Sometimes in Paul's letters, he will say that he is just giving advice and not commanding concerning a certain topic. Is that message still inspired?

2. The Psalms often speak of the writer wanting to kill the foes of God, sometimes in a horrible fashion. Is this just an accurate history of Israel's war-poetry, or are these imprecatory Psalms God-breathed?

3. Some parts of the Bible are poetic when speaking of events in the far past or far future. Are these passages, though unclear, God-breathed? Or just a holy history of what people thought about God?

28

The Bible and Apologetics (Part 3)

MESSAGE INTRODUCTION

People grow and change. All of us are quite different than we were when we were younger, or than when we first were converted. But not all change is good. Some depart from the basics of the faith, and they do so because they fail to submit to Jesus' right to guide us in our system of beliefs. Jesus saves us, but after that, it is up to us to figure things out—or so we think. In this lecture, R.C. will show how the lordship of Christ and the Bible relate, and how this impacts our apologetics.

In the third of five lectures from Dr. Sproul, he will:

- Establish a solid starting point for using the Bible (26)
- Establish its normative authority (27)
- **Establish a noncircular principle of self-attestation (28)**
- Discuss the doctrine of inspiration and address Barth's critique (29)
- Introduce us to John Calvin's teaching on the authority of Scripture (30)

LEARNING OBJECTIVES

1. To be introduced to the important work of the International Council on Biblical Inerrancy.
2. To be able to show a relationship between Christ and the Bible without arguing in a circle.
3. To question the need for the tension liberals face between claiming Jesus as Lord yet questioning the Bible.

QUOTATIONS AND THOUGHTS

If you want to interpret well and confidently, set Christ before you, for He is the man to whom it all applies, every bit of it. (Martin Luther)

The Jesus of the New Testament has at least one advantage over the Jesus of modern construction—He is real. (J. Gresham Machen)

There is nothing holier, or better, or safer, than to content ourselves with the authority of Christ alone. (John Calvin)

LECTURE OUTLINE

I. The International Council on Biblical Inerrancy
   a. Surprisingly, the lordship of Christ played a great part in scholars' trust in the Bible.
   b. But isn't this a circular argument? If the Bible is the only place you can find that Jesus taught that the Bible was God's Word, isn't Jesus' testimony invalid as a positive argument for the truth of the Bible?

II. How are the lordship of Christ and the Bible related?
   a. Illustration: An old friend in Philadelphia
   b. Jesus is Lord of all, including what we think about the Bible.

III. The Argument for the Bible
   a. Premise: The Bible is a basically trustworthy historical document.
      i. This is where you start with non-Christians.
      ii. With Christians or in the church, for different reasons, you start at the same place.
      iii. There are rules that establish trustworthiness, rules that are agreed upon and applied to Josephus, Tacitus, Herodotus, and so on. There are standards relating to internal and external coherence.
      iv. Illustration: Sir Ramsey's study of Luke's historicity
      v. In fact, at no time in history has the basic historical reliability of the Bible been more clear and established than today.
      vi. See F.F. Bruce's booklet, "The New Testament Documents: Are They Reliable?" for a more detailed summary of this point.
   b. Premise: The Bible is suitable to make a reasonable judgment about the person of Jesus of Nazareth.
   c. Premise: Jesus claimed to be more than a man. He claimed to have great authority. But let's assume that He was only a prophet (as many religions acknowledge, and nothing more (at this point).
   d. The Question: What did Jesus believe about the Bible?

The Bible and Apologetics (Part 3)

      e. Thus, you start with basic reliability, move to solid information about Jesus, then make the inquiry, "What was Jesus' view of Scripture?"

IV. Tension in Biblical Scholarship
      a. Many scholars want to have it both ways; they want to acknowledge the basic reliability of the Bible, put their trust in Christ, but then attack the Bible that Jesus authoritatively blessed.
      b. Some claim that Jesus, in touching His humanity, could not have known how flawed the Bible was.
      c. In the church, the argument for the Bible is actually an argument for Christ.

STUDY QUESTIONS

1. Define a circular argument.

2. Outline R.C.'s three-step argument for the authority of Scripture.

DISCUSSION QUESTIONS

1. Do you believe that the Bible is God-breathed (2 Timothy 3)? Why or why not?

2. Do you see a way to resolve the tension between not believing that the Bible is inerrant yet maintaining that Jesus is trustworthy?

3. Is the inerrancy of Scripture a fundamental of the faith? Before you answer, note that inerrancy is not a part of any creed of the church. And notice that it is not a part of any Gospel presentation in the Bible (such as Acts 2).

29

The Bible and Apologetics (Part 4)

MESSAGE INTRODUCTION

How could Jesus be God, and yet make mistakes in His statements? Karl Barth thinks he found a way to save Jesus' reputation, yet at the expense of the Scripture's infallibility. R.C. disagrees, and this lecture will show you why.

In the fourth of five lectures from Dr. Sproul, he will:

- Establish a solid starting point for using the Bible (26)
- Establish its normative authority (27)
- Establish a noncircular principle of self-attestation (28)
- **Discuss the doctrine of inspiration and address Barth's critique (29)**
- Introduce us to John Calvin's teaching on the authority of Scripture (30)

LEARNING OBJECTIVES

1. To be able to discuss the doctrine of communicable and incommunicable attributes.
2. To be introduced to the heresy of Docetism, or that Jesus only appeared to be human.
3. To be able to show how Karl Barth errs in arguing for the humanity of Christ, enabling Him to be less than perfect in His estimation of Scripture.

QUOTATIONS AND THOUGHTS

Every virtue known to man is found in Jesus. (Michael Green)

The Bible and Apologetics (Part 4)

The more you know about Jesus, the less you will be satisfied with superficial views of Him. (C.H. Spurgeon)

Christ is the most unique person in history. No man can write a history of the human race without giving first and foremost place to the penniless teacher of Nazareth. (H.G. Wells)

LECTURE OUTLINE

I. Scholars have tried to resolve the tension between Christ and Scripture.
   a. If Jesus is perfect, then His testimony concerning Scripture is also perfect.
   b. But if it can be shown that Jesus' humanity could err (not being omniscient), and that from that, Jesus could be wrong about the Bible and remain deity and the Lord of the Christian faith, then this tension can be resolved (at the expense of both Jesus and the Bible).

II. Communicable and Incommunicable Attributes
   a. Some traits of God can also exist in man, such as love or anger.
   b. Others cannot, such as omniscience, omnipotence, or immensity.
   c. The Council of Chalcedon in 451 declared that there was to be no mixing of the natures of Christ. This was to counter Docetism, a heresy that declared that Jesus only appeared human.

III. Karl Barth and Inerrancy
   a. With this history, Barth wanted to say that Jesus, as touching His humanity, was not omniscient. True. But then Barth wanted to assert that His humanity could fail.
   b. Is it a sin to be wrong, especially if you have no way to know any better?
   c. Illustration: R.C. in the Classroom
   d. But Jesus claimed to teach with the highest authority possible, the highest amount of certitude conceivable.
   e. This "solution" may address some problems, but it makes much worse ones.
   f. Barth called the doctrine of inspiration "Biblical Docetism."
   g. "To err is human."

IV. The *Words* of God, Not the *Word* of God
   a. Many would say that the Bible is not God's Word, but contains God's Word.
   b. The Holy Spirit takes the human words and makes them powerful, makes them become the Word to us.
   c. But the question remains: How can that which is God's Word err?

STUDY QUESTIONS

1. What is the tension between Christ and the Bible that modern scholars have struggled over?

2. How have they, most notably Karl Barth, tried to resolve it?

3. What problems does that solution create?

4. Does the Bible "becoming" God's Word solve the problem? Why?

DISCUSSION QUESTIONS

1. Read Psalm 119. What "adjustments" would a modern liberal have to make to its language?

2. If Jesus is still incarnate, and therefore still has a human nature, using the logic of Karl Barth, could Jesus still be making mistakes in heaven?

3. Read the text from the Council of Chalcedon supplied below. Imagine yourself in the early church, battling Docetists. How would you have answered them?

DEFINITION OF CHALCEDON (451 A.D.):

Therefore, following the holy fathers, we all with one accord teach men to acknowledge one and the same Son, our Lord Jesus Christ, at once complete in Godhead and complete in manhood, truly God and truly man, consisting also of a reasonable soul and body; of one substance with the Father as regards his Godhead, and at the same time of one substance with us as regards his manhood; like us in all respects, apart from sin; as regards his Godhead, begotten of the Father before the ages, but yet as regards his manhood begotten, for us men and for our salvation, of Mary the Virgin, the God-bearer; one and the same Christ, Son, Lord, Only-begotten, recognized in two natures, without confusion, without change, without division, without separation; the distinction of natures being in no way annulled by the union, but rather the characteristics of each nature being preserved and coming together to form one person and subsistence, not as parted or separated into two persons, but one and the same Son and Only-begotten God the Word, Lord Jesus Christ; even as the prophets from earliest times spoke of him, and our Lord Jesus Christ himself taught us, and the creed of the fathers has handed down to us.

30

The Bible and Apologetics (Part 5)

MESSAGE INTRODUCTION

What makes the Bible "the Bible"? Is it just announcing it so? If that were true, the world would be filled with "holy" books. John Calvin's study of the Bible points to the unique properties and claims of the Bible that put it head and shoulders above any other book that claims to be from God.

In the fifth of five lectures from Dr. Sproul, he will:

- Establish a solid starting point for using the Bible (26)
- Establish its normative authority (27)
- Establish a noncircular principle of self-attestation (28)
- Discuss the doctrine of inspiration and address Barth's critique (29)
- **Introduce us to John Calvin's teaching on the authority of Scripture (30)**

LEARNING OBJECTIVES

1. To be introduced to the scholarship of John Calvin on Scripture.
2. To become familiar with terms such as "indicia, "heavenliness," "the ring of truth," and "morality" as applied to the Holy Scriptures.
3. To understand the means used by the Holy Spirit to encourage our respect for God's Word.

QUOTATIONS AND THOUGHTS

God's chosen instrument of our conversion is His Word, not our reasoning ability. (Will Metzger)

The Word is both a glass to show us the spots of our soul and a laver to wash them away. (Thomas Watson)

The fundamental mode whereby our rational Creator guides His rational creatures is by rational understanding and application of His written Word. (J.I. Packer)

LECTURE OUTLINE

I. The Authority of Scripture
   a. John Calvin's *Institutes* offered some unique arguments for the authority of Scripture.
   b. Calvin looked at the internal evidence for the authority of Scripture.
   c. These attributes are known as indicia.

II. Calvin's *Indicia*
   a. Calvin said that the Scriptures have existed for many, many years. No book has been subjected to such supernatural care during such a variety of attacks. (Remember that Calvin made this comment in the 16th century.)
   b. Calvin referred to a quality of Scripture known as *The Heavenliness of the Matter*.
   c. The discipline of philosophy prepares the student to critically analyze ideas and documents. Philosophy must be read with a comb, keeping the truth and casting away the trash. Scripture is, rather than being read critically, reading us critically. Its depth and scope are what Calvin noted as being a profound proof of its truth.
   d. Illustration: Samuel and Eli and the Word of God
   e. Calvin noted the lack of internal contradiction and intricate unity of Scripture.
   f. The morality of Scripture is also astounding. It is filled with high justice and great mercy, and humans know innately (as Kant discusses) that moral codes are good and right.
   g. Internally, the Bible specifically predicts events that are then accurately fulfilled in the future, affirmed by external sources. Just the prophecies relating to Jesus Christ in the Old Testament, which are fulfilled in the New, are unspeakable "long shots." It is quite unlikely that even one would be fulfilled, but they all are fulfilled in Christ.

III. The Limits of Internal Evidence
   a. These testimonies are suitable to stop the mouths of those who would oppose the Bible, the "obstreperous."
   b. But they fall short of having the power to convert unregenerate minds to God. This remains the purview of the Holy Spirit alone.

> c. The Holy Spirit, Calvin summarizes, causes the unbeliever to surrender to the *indicia*.

STUDY QUESTIONS

1. What are some internal evidences for the integrity and authority of Scripture?

2. What was the word Calvin used to describe these evidences?

3. What are the limits of internal evidence?

DISCUSSION QUESTIONS

1. What about the Bible strikes you as being most impressive?

2. What about the Bible is most disturbing to you?

3. Why does it take a work of the Holy Spirit to surrender to the *indicia*? Look at Ephesians 2:1-10 for some hints.

31

The Deity of Christ

MESSAGE INTRODUCTION

What do you do with Jesus? That is the fundamental question that apologetics enable to be humbly and logically asked of the unbeliever. But what do you do when religious people disagree on the answer?

Christians can disagree on many questions, but the nature and divinity of Christ is not among them. The church agrees on the deity of Christ for good reasons, and these will be discussed by Dr. Sproul in this last lecture prior to the *Question and Answer* section.

LEARNING OBJECTIVES

1. To discuss the meaning of the term "worldview."
2. To understand the purpose of proving the existence of God and the authority of Scripture.
3. To be able to answer the question, "Is Jesus God?" on the basis of these assumptions.

QUOTATIONS AND THOUGHTS

Jesus Christ is God in the form of man; as completely God as if He were not man; as completely man as if He were not God. (A.J.F. Behrends)

Remember, Christ was not a deified man, neither was he a humanized God. He was perfectly God and man at the same time. (C.H. Spurgeon)

The Son of God did not unite Himself with a human person, but with a human nature. (Charles Hodge)

The Deity of Christ

LECTURE OUTLINE

I. The Two Issues
   a. Does God exist?
   b. Is the Bible the Word of God?

II. The Consequences
   a. Your answers to the previous two questions determine how you live and value people.
   b. Your answers to the previous questions either put you at odds with the world or put you in line with the world.
   c. Understanding the relationship of the Bible and natural revelation enables us to think God's thoughts and see the imprint of the Creator in nature.
   d. Is God's Word the final authority for how we live?
   e. And if it is our authority in every matter, how we interpret the Bible matters. Our hermeneutic matters to God.
   f. Illustration: Sproul vs. MacArthur on Baptism
   g. Illustration: Sproul and Abortion

III. The Deity of Christ: An Essential of the Faith
   a. John 1:1 teaches that Jesus is God, yet a distinct person in the Godhead.
   b. In what sense was Jesus "with" God?
      i. *"Sun"*
      ii. *"Para" or "Meta"*
      iii. *"Pros"*
   c. This is not the only text but was the major text that the church studied for hundreds of years to clarify the nature of Christ.
   d. Apologetics can go to the New Testament and give a defense of Jesus' deity based on it because the basic reliability of the Bible has been established, along with its authority. Once the Scriptures are established, we can go to them to settle controversies.

STUDY QUESTIONS

1. What are the two main questions that this series has addressed?

2. What is a worldview?

3. How does John 1 demonstrate that Jesus is deity? Find at least five proofs from this chapter.

DISCUSSION QUESTIONS

1. Have you ever talked to anyone who denied that Jesus was God, and even used the Bible to attempt to debate the point? How did you respond? How would you respond now, after hearing this series?

2. Does this series give you an idea of what areas you need to work on in your apologetics or evangelism? Explain

3. List three people you know with whom you want to have apologetical and evangelistic conversations. Pray that these conversations will happen over the next few weeks, and ask your friends to pray with you for these people and for yourself.

32

Questions and Answers

MESSAGE INTRODUCTION

After we completed the lecture portion of the *Defending Your Faith* series with Dr. R.C. Sproul, we asked our studio audience if they had any questions. The questions that R.C. hears are uncut and unrehearsed and as always, his answers are very helpful.

LEARNING OBJECTIVE

- To gain practical insights on apologetics through a question-and-answer session.

QUOTATIONS AND THOUGHTS

The real mark of a saint is that he makes it easier for others to believe in God. (Anon.)

The real problem of Christianity is not atheism or skepticism, but the non-witnessing Christian trying to smuggle his own soul into heaven. (J.S. Stewart)

LECTURE OUTLINE

Question 1:

Question 2:

Question 3:

Question 4:

Question 5:

Question 6:

Question 7:

STUDY AND DISCUSSION QUESTIONS

1. What was your favorite question? Why?

2. What other questions did this lecture raise in your mind? Write them below.

FOR ADDITIONAL READING

These books are not without their faults, nor are the authors. But all of them are useful in building your ability to defend your faith if read critically and compared with Scripture.

Michael J. Behe. *Darwin's Black Box: The Biochemical Challenge to Evolution* (New York: Free Press, 1996)

Phillip E. Johnson. *Defeating Darwinism by Opening Minds* (Downers Grove, Ill.: InterVarsity Press, 1997)

J.P. Moreland, ed. *The Creation Hypotheses: Scientific Evidence for an Intelligent Designer* (Downers Grove, Ill.: InterVarsity Press, 1994)

D.A. Carson, *The Gagging of God* (Grand Rapids: Zondervan, 1995)

Gene Edward Veith Jr. *Postmodern Times* (Wheaton, Ill.: Crossway, 1995)

Gordon H. Clark. *Thales to Dewey*, 2nd ed. (Unicoi, Tenn.: The Trinity Foundation, 1989)

Thomas Aquinas. *Summa Theologica: A Concise Translation* (Allen, Tex.: Christian Classics, 1997)

Peter Kreeft. *Summa of the Summa* (San Fransisco: Ignatius Press, 1990)

Peter Kreeft and R.K. Tacelli. *Handbook of Christian Apologetics* (Downers Grove, Ill.: InterVarsity Press, 1994)

Frederick C. Copleston, *A History of Philosophy* (Westminster, Md.: Newman Press, 1962)

Aristotle. *A New Aristotle Reader* (Princeton, N.J.: Princeton University Press, 1987)

Steven Cowan, ed. *Five Views on Apologetics* (Grand Rapids: Zondervan, 2000)

Francis A. Schaeffer, *Three Essential Books in 1 Volume (The God Who is There, Escape from Reason, He is There and He is not Silent)* (Wheaton, Ill.: Crossway, 1990)

R.C. Sproul, John Gerstner, Art Lindsley. *Classical Apologetics* (Grand Rapids: Zondervan, 1984)